HOME OF THE BRAVE

HOME OF THE BRAVE

A Guided Journal for Promoting
God, Family, and Country—
At Home and in the World

THE DEPLORABLE CHOIR

BOMBARDIER
BOOKS

A BOMBARDIER BOOKS BOOK
An Imprint of Post Hill Press

Home of the Brave:
A Guided Journal for Promoting God, Family, and Country—At Home and in the World
© 2020 by The Deplorable Choir
All Rights Reserved

ISBN: 978-1-64293-550-9

Cover photo by Cory Morris

Post Hill Press
New York • Nashville
posthillpress.com

Published in the United States of America

TABLE OF CONTENTS

INTRODUCTION

Who Are the Ladies of The Deplorable Choir?

In 2016, I (Cjaye) felt helpless. I was on the Trump train from the moment I watched Trump take the ride down the escalator to announce his candidacy. Then I was shocked at how many people were attacking and railing against this great man who clearly loved our country. I thought, "I've got to do something but I'm completely unqualified. I'm not smart enough. I'm just a stay-at-home mom with no credentials." It all seemed unjust and I felt my fighting side start to rise up and gain strength. I took to social media, as many of us do when we have something to say. I remember comparing Trump to King David in the Bible on one post. Oh, the reaction I received. My friends argued with me or just brushed me off with a laugh and a few "You're so cute" comments. I felt deflated. In my living room with Lynz and Val, I swore I would never do that again—until I would do it, again and again!

Fast-forward to February 2017, when our favorite general, General Flynn, was fired as national security advisor. I had an odd feeling and thought, "Something stinks enough to make a maggot gag." I couldn't put my finger on it, but that's the moment I decided I better start paying attention to what's going on in this country. I started digging into everything:

the Russia connection, Comey, Clapper, the FBI star-crossed lover texts of Strzok and Page—all of the buzz—and realized there was a real coalition forming against President Trump! They were setting him up and it seemed as obvious as the nose on your face. But the talking points of the mainstream media and the left tried to give legitimacy to what so many of us knew as the beginning of the biggest scam in American history! I was fired up, but once again, I did not know what I could do aside from a few Facebook posts, where I would just get in fights with friends.

The vitriol and viciousness continued to grow. The left got louder and leaned so far to the left that they were about to fall over. But the majority on the right stayed silent. Why? Then it occurred to me that it probably wasn't because they *wanted* to remain silent. They were like me and had no idea how to become involved. We watch the entertainment industry create a culture we don't relate to and feel helpless. We watch our government rip apart our Constitution and we feel defenseless. We watch scrooges try to rip apart our Christian roots and the very fabric our nation was built upon and we feel overwhelmed. How do you go up against the machine that feels like it's out to rip apart the American values we grew up with? It feels impossible.

When it came to the political process, I was like a deer in headlights, but that burn in my belly to do something grew. I no longer cared if I was the perfect person, if I was among the highest educated; I just decided to go for it!

I grabbed by best friend Val and my sister Lyndsey, and we raised our voices together and sang! Yes, this was completely unconventional, and not really the way I would encourage others to speak up, but nonetheless we did something. We didn't care that we were far from perfect and didn't really know how to write songs. But, gosh darn it, we were going to write some songs for our president. We didn't really care what people thought; we just hoped our music would bring joy, laughter, and fun to a demographic that to up until this point had been demonized. We are happy to let people laugh at our expense! So, yes, my kids are crying in the background of some of our videos. And yes, Val and Lyndsey had never cracked a note in their life. We didn't care; we just did it.

The result? We've been able to reach millions of people. We even had the opportunity to sing the national anthem in front of tens of thousands of people at the Toyota Center in Houston for a Trump rally! We also got to sing at a Dallas rally and ended up on Fox News after one of our videos went viral. We like to think we have been a little bright spot for many in what often feels like a dark time. We've made people laugh and along the way, we hope we've influenced many people to be brave, speak up, and do something.

Why This Book?

We believe our founding fathers intended for those representing our country to be regular people. *For the people by the people, baby!* We continue to be inspired by the stories of other people who, regardless of how "equipped" they are, just step out and do something. We have a friend, Terrence Williams, who posted a video of himself eating fried chicken one night talking of his love for President Trump; it went viral. Not because it was the most eloquent speech, but because he said what he wanted to say, and people connected to it. He was just being himself, funny as H-E-double hockey sticks and eating chicken. The rest is history. And when Scott Presler recognized that every vote counted, he went door to door to help people register to vote. He did this out of love for his country and nothing more! There are so many other stories like these that remind us everyone is capable of influence and every voice can make a difference. Regular, everyday people. We also know many may feel overwhelmed and helpless, like we did. So, we wrote *Home of the Brave* to encourage other patriotic moms to embrace their spirit, find their voice, and raise their families as proud Americans. From home, to community, to country, we want this book to be the inspiration you've been searching for to create and live your American dream.

How to Use This Book

If you haven't noticed yet, this book is organized into three sections: your home, your community and your country. It made sense to us to start small and safe in your own home, then build your courageous, patriotic lifestyle out from there, right? With each section, we have a few chapters on ways you can find your voice, claim your true spirit and speak out—loud and proud! Then, we've added some of our ideas on how to do those things. These ideas come from our own lives and what we've done (or are doing, or are planning to do). And, if you accidently think we're perfect, we share some of our spectacular fails along the way!

We also know that every mom is super busy and needs to take things in stages. That's why our ideas come in two steps: baby steps and big steps. We thought about how our kids started out with baby steps long before they could make big steps. Isn't that true for everything with kids, from actually learning to walk to finding their own strengths and passions? Baby steps first, then big steps! Why not allow that same grace for yourself? So, the baby steps are easy things to do that don't take a lot of time, energy or money to implement. The big steps, once you're ready, will take you a bit more commitment, follow-through, and courage in sharing your voice. There are no rules here, so pick and choose what works for you when it works for you!

With each idea or activity, we've also added a few blank notes pages. Why? Because we want this to work for you! Our ideas are just a jumping-off point, and we know that some of you amazing MAGA moms out there will have some cool ideas of your own. So, use the note pages to jot down your own ideas, maybe stick in a picture or two of your patriotic home—or the one you love from some Pinterest site—and share some accomplishments you've made. Make this a reference book for yourself as you build your own *Home of the Brave*!

How to Get Started

You know that first chance we had to sing the national anthem in front of a huge crowd of people? We had never done anything like that before—ever! Were we nervous? Nervous enough to sneak in a flask of tequila that fell out on the ground as we met Lara Trump for the first time, but we just put on our MAGA hats, stepped up on stage, and did it. We let go of perfection a long time ago and decided that no matter what we did, we would do it with heart. You may never sing the national anthem at an event, but you can sing it for your kids and sing it in the shower! You may do something small, like put that Trump bumper sticker on your car or put that MAGA hat on your head. Whatever you do, we want you to say, "Screw perfection," and just go for it. No one cares if you have a Harvard degree or any degree for that matter. No one cares if you have major funding and donors or if you're so poor you don't have a pot to piss in or a window to throw it out of. *What you do have is a love of God, country, and family. So, let's do the dang thing!*

YOUR HOME

CHAPTER ONE

CULTIVATING A PATRIOTIC SPIRIT: IT STARTS AT HOME

*"A love for tradition has never weakened a nation,
indeed it has strengthened nations in their hour of peril."*

—WINSTON S. CHURCHILL

All too often, people keep the very essence of their being hidden in their heart. We've become so conditioned to not only worry about what others think of us, of our opinions, and of how we live our lives, but we've also convinced ourselves that by fitting in we can somehow stay in our safe zone. These days, it's very much the path of least resistance—zip our lips, put on a mask, and blend in with the crowd rather than to show off what is in our soul. But what if that silence is what got us in the mess our country is in in the first place? A country where our crosses are torn down. Where our history is erased. Where our kids are taught that genders are like Baskin Robbins' thirty-one flavors and they can be whichever one strikes their fancy at the drop of a hat. It seems that American history and patriotic traditions are being ripped apart and taken away from many aspects of our lifestyle. Things that used to be common occurrences—like standing for the national anthem—are looked down on and are sometimes even vilified!

The good news is that things can change. Your home is a place where, if you've been silent in the past, you can feel free to begin to cultivate the patriotic spirit you may have kept locked inside for far too long. Home is a place where you can create traditions and rituals that will not only help you take small steps to finding that big voice we know you have, but a place where you can instill that big voice in your children. Not only can you do this, it's an opportunity you should not miss. Our kids are thrown into a world where they are forced to process more information than ever before in human history. With the internet and social media, they are exposed to an exciting world full of contrasting and differing opinions and cultures than our own, so it's more important than ever to give them a firm foundation. We in no way believe in being helicopter parents or shielding them from the outside world, but we know the importance of planting those seeds in good soil. You know the old saying, "You can lead a horse to water, but you can't make him drink"? Well it's our job as parents to lovingly lead our "little horses" to the water.

Ever since Trump ran for office, we have jokingly referred to ourselves as MAGA moms, and for MAGA moms like us, home is where patriotism begins. We believe that God is the foundation for a healthy home and family, and faithful families are the backbone of our nation. If you watch any news these days, and really, it's impossible not to, you may feel the need to find a dark closet and take cover. Morals and values have been completely obliterated. There are no constants anymore, everything is subjective, people are adherent to whatever whim tickles their fancy, and the PC culture is out of control. There are no safe spaces for us folks; that is what the leftists do. MAGA moms act, and this is why making your home a safe haven for tradition, faith, and patriotism is more important than ever. In thought, word, and deed, staying true to your values matters most inside your own walls. Home is where the heart is, and we want to help you show your true heart: your patriotic heart!

Let's start with things you can do around your home to remind your-self of your own beliefs and share them with your family. Some of the ideas may seem simple, or obvious, but let's be honest: when you are a busy MAGA mom, it's sometimes the simple, small, and obvious things that are the first to fly out the window. For example, it should be obvious for our kids to always have shoes on their feet when they walk into a public place, but that doesn't always happen in our households. Heck, they're lucky if they have pants on at times. Whether it's what they see you do or what you say, you're giving your family something they're not getting in the outside world. Having habits, traditions, and rituals, no matter how big or small, will instill important core values in your household. Your family will benefit from a solid understanding of the importance of God, family, and country—and that's stability. When children have a stable home and strong values, they feel safe and more confident—ready to take on the world.

Things to Do

As you read this section and review these activities and ideas, remember what we said in the introduction about baby steps and big steps. We know everyone is not in the same place, so just do what works for you. Whether you're a loud and proud MAGA MOM or a quieter maga mom, you are already amazing! Our hope is that these ideas will spark something inside of you, give you some inspiration, and provide an opportunity for you to show your true, patriotic heart. Also, as moms, we understand that you are more often than not pressed for time, money, and space. That's the other reason we have both baby steps and big steps.

BaBy StEpS

These are little things you can do: thoughts, actions, and even a little decorating, that don't take any effort, time, or money but really can set the tone and spirit for your home. You don't have to buy anything or make anything (unless you want to). These are just fun little activities or items that show off your faith and patriotism, and hopefully are the building blocks of what will grow into a love of God and country for your kids as well.

Display Your Colors

Maybe you fly your American flag on the 4th of July, but why not more often? Let your flag fly on Veterans Day, Voting Day, Memorial Day! Fly it every day of the year like we do, if you want. Remember, even if you live somewhere where passersby don't see it, fly it anyway. This is for you, your heart, and your family. Besides, we personally love the Americana style and think it makes our homes much cuter. Do you have other items in your home that represent your patriotic spirit: a star-patterned platter or red, white and blue throw pillows? Well, get those babies out and leave them out! We're not talking about hanging bunting out your window and painting your walls like Old Glory, but maybe there's a place where you can leave those red, white and blue pillows out all year long!

Leave Your Bible on the Table

If your faith is the foundation of who you are and the life you want to lead, be sure you keep that front and center. Wherever you have your devotional, your quiet time with God, leave the Bible out for every family member to see. We know that quiet time with God is done by yourself, but without saying a word, you can remind yourself and others that God's word matters in your home.

Sing Patriotic Songs

This one is personal for us. Obviously, you don't need to film yourself and put it on the internet like we do, but nothing stirs the heart and sets the tone of a home like music. An easy way to cultivate a patriotic heart in a child is to teach them the songs we grew up with. "You're a Grand Old Flag," "America the Beautiful," "God Bless America," and of course, the national anthem are good starters. Sing them in the car, sing them around the house, and you can be sure your kids will grow up knowing them by heart. I have a friend who sings the national anthem to her kids as a lullaby. As funny as it sounds, it is just a little thing that will be instilled in them for years to come! And come on, who could take a knee during a song your mother sang you to sleep with?

Buy a MAGA Hat

If you don't already have one (we have several) but want one, buy a MAGA hat today! That's all, just buy it. We understand that some people are nervous or unsure about wearing it out in public. Of course, there are horror stories about people being beaten up just for wearing one, but you would be surprised how much support we get from wearing ours in public. We frequently get high-fives, free food, and a whole lot of "Thank yous!" Our crazy selves even wore them in downtown San Francisco! We received nothing but love, people. But remember, just get the hat, then you can leave it on the counter or hang it on your coat rack and work your way up to wearing it around the house or in the yard. That's all for now—this just about what happens in your home.

BiG StEpS

These ideas take a bit more planning and some interaction with your family, which is a good thing. However, we get that it may take you more time to get something going. Depending on your family dynamic, you may get a little resistance to making changes to things as usual. Don't worry about a few misses and do not strive for perfection. Just pick one of these ideas (or one of your own) to connect with your family, start sharing your beliefs, and start making memories. The overall idea here is to be present with each other without the distraction of the outside world. Here are a few ideas we try to practice:

Have a No-Phone Zone

Technology is everywhere, and it serves a purpose, but we like to refer to those little hunks of metal we carry around with half-eaten apples on the back, "moment stealers." Nothing beats connecting with your family IRL (in real life), but those little suckers sure know how to distract you from doing just that! Why not have a place in your home, or a time in your day, where no phones or technology are allowed? It sounds simple enough, but we know this can be a big step in many households. We're all so accustomed to having our phones at the ready for social media, texting, downloading, and streaming that our kids can barely communicate without them. Still, it's important to truly connect with your children and be present in those moments with them, and it's nearly impossible to do that when everyone is staring at their phone screens. Whether it's no phones before leaving for school, or during homework time, or at the dinner table, find a place and time that works for your family to unplug from the outside world and plug into what matters most. Now, you can share your thoughts and feelings, ask your kids about their day, what they're hearing "out there" and how they feel about things.

Have Real Family Dinners

We cannot emphasize this one enough. Okay, we're about to throw a hard fact at you, but we're all tough here and can handle it, right? Kids who have family dinners less than three times a week are more likely to abuse prescription drugs than kids who have frequent family dinners! So, as impossible as it may be to fit in with everyone's busy schedules, make that effort. It may not happen every week or with every family member present, but set a goal to have this time to gather. Family dinner is an ideal time to talk with your children—and everyone in your home. You can incorporate little memorable rituals by having a theme night for certain nights of the week. Don't overcomplicate this one, just pick something easy and fun. One night can be pizza night where you play games at the table. How about a movie night where you eat dinner on the couch? Or just have that dinner together, because just getting everyone around the table at the same time can be its own feat! The important thing here is that you have a topic or question that everyone discusses. One of our favorite topics is American history, like "today in history." It doesn't matter if anyone has the answers; asking one or two questions about a specific event or person can be a great conversation starter. If you're not sure where to begin, buy a conversation starter game—or look them up on the internet if you're strapped for cash. You will find so many different categories and topics that will help keep dinner fun and memorable. And, these little habits can become family traditions that share your values in a fun way.

Have a Daily Devotional with Your Kids

One way to keep your faith at the center of your home is to have a plan for reading Bible verses. Every morning (or as many as we can muster), we have a devotional with our kids. For your little ones, you can read a verse to them and share what it means. If they're old enough, have them read the verse and then ask them to share what they think it means and how it applies to their life today. Another time you can make this happen is in the car as you drive your children to school or soccer practice or whatever. Just share the verse and let the conversation start. Please don't stress about getting this done every day; just begin to plant seeds around your faith.

Share Your Gratitude

We've all heard about gratitude journals, and maybe you are already doing this or have tried it. However, the difference here is that we want you to focus on your gratitude for being an American. There are no rules for doing this every day or having a certain number of things on a list. Just think about the freedoms you enjoy, opportunities you have, and reasons you love this country. It can be big things, like the freedom to worship as you wish, or little things, like the variety of landscapes and climates we have. Your children may not know, or may take for granted, some of the benefits and joys unique to American life, so start sharing with them. Each time you have something you're grateful for, share it with your kids. You can even use it as a conversation starter on freedoms they enjoy. Now, you don't even have to write anything down for this, but you can if you want to. We've even given you some pages at the end of this chapter to do just that!

Comments from the Choir

We realize that some of this stuff might seem like no-brainers, but even in our families, with the constant hustle and bustle and high demands, the little things get lost in the blur of daily life. We get so busy with getting through the day that being with our kids isn't always what we hope it will be. We all need to be reminded of the importance of sharing our values with our family. There are so many studies that emphasize the importance of rituals and family traditions. They are the memories that give your family magic, give your kids their identity and confidence, and hopefully will help them navigate the world when they leave your home. So, even if some of these ideas might seem obvious, we wanted to share them with you. This also seems like a good time to remind you that we don't care if you do things perfectly; heck, we've literally never done anything perfectly. This isn't a book about perfection, but our hope is to encourage others to take steps and strengthen your family's patriotic spirit. It really does all start at home; make yours matter!

Notes

Notes

Notes

Notes

CHAPTER TWO

FINDING YOUR VOICE WITH FAMILY AND FRIENDS

"If tolerance, respect and equity permeate family life, they will translate into values that shape societies, nations and the world."

—KOFI ANNAN

If home is truly the heart of the family, as we believe, then this is where you first start to find your voice as well—beyond singing patriotic songs in your living room with your kids.

You might think we come from a family full of conservatives, but the complete opposite is true. We are a big mush pot of political opinions; to be honest, whose family isn't? One of our favorite pastimes is traveling up to Minnesota to spend time with our super liberal family. Even at a young age, we could feel the excitement building up in the car on the way to our aunt's house just knowing a huge debate was about to transpire. We were always in awe of our Dad's eagerness to walk into the living room, be covered with kisses from the five super-loving aunts that would greet us, and then have the most epic political throwdown. We can still remember our mom on absolute nerve-racking edge and shooting threatening glares at him across the room the moment he would break the ice with some big conservative talking point. It was her nightmare. It was our Disneyland.

They would go back and forth with such ferociousness that you would think these people would never speak again. Instead it always ended in hugs, food, and Christmas carols. It was so strange, but so wonderful. We loved knowing at a young age that it was okay to have different opinions, disagree on them, but still love each other. And honestly, probably zero people will be on board with us on this, but we loved how explosive it all was. It was like I was watching a good reality TV show but in our own living room and it always had a happy ending. This is probably where our love for drama was born.

Obviously, not everyone's family is like this. Not everyone enjoys the back and forth of a good old fight and debate. A lot of people have true family divisions for even sharing their political stance but, growing up seeing both sides, we think it's so important to be able to share what is important to you and share it in a loving way where people can find common ground. That makes sense and sounds easy enough, but how many times have you tried to express yourself only to be shut down by someone in your family? We think one of the biggest misconceptions in this ever-so-divided culture is that you can't have conversations with your friends who disagree with you politically. Even worse is the idea that you can't be friends with someone who disagrees with you politically. That is insane and just strengthens the division among Americans. If we are unable to have productive conversations, how is anyone ever going to find common ground?

We know speaking up isn't easy. More than once, when we have felt brave enough to share our voices—and no matter how strongly we felt or no matter how prepared we thought we were—we were challenged. Immediately, we felt the blood rushing to our faces and our hearts pounding in our chests and wished we had just kept our big mouths shut. Obviously, that didn't stop us for long, but we understand how you might feel. We realize this is a step a lot of people are unwilling to take, but there are ways you can talk to people that help them let their guard down and—believe it or not—have productive conversations.

So, even if you're the only MAGA mom at the Thanksgiving table, feel free to be yourself. Don't feel you have to hold back who you are because of what someone else thinks of you. We're not saying that you should intentionally bring strife to the dinner table, but remember you're also teaching your children to find and use their voices, too. It can sometimes be the smallest voice that makes the biggest difference. We recently had the opportunity to meet Scott Presler. More and more people are hearing about this conservative activist who is literally cleaning up crap off the street in San Francisco, Baltimore, and every other dirty liberal town across the nation. Scott started as one person heading to Baltimore to clean up one street, and now he has people across the country helping him pick up trash—tons of trash. He said something that really struck a chord with us, "A loud minority is more powerful than a silent majority." We know everyone says, "Liberals are loud, but conservatives speak with their vote." And although that is true, that will not save our culture, and in the long run, it will fail us all. Clearly, staying in our safe zone isn't what we should be doing. We've got voices; let's put those babies to work! Think about it: in a few short decades, a loud and obnoxious minority (ahem, celebrities) was able to fundamentally change the very fabric of our nation. What will they be able to accomplish if we don't learn to lovingly use our voice to spread our beliefs, values, and other things we hold true to our hearts? We really should bring the same fire to the defense of things we hold dear as the left does, or else, we will cease to exist. Dennis Prager says in his book *Exodus*, "There are far more kind and honest people than there are courageous people. Unfortunately, however, in the battle against evil, all the good traits in the world amount to little when not accompanied by courage." Our hope is we all can begin to find the courage that is within us to speak up, so we start to make the difference we know a collective of voices can.

Things to Do

Now is the time to focus on sharing your patriotic, God-fearing, country-loving, Trump-supporting voice. We want to offer a few ideas and things we've learned along the way to make it easier and, hopefully, a little less scary. It's okay to start small and wait for your courage to catch up to your heart. Remember, this chapter is just about finding your voice with family and friends. We are not asking you to make a speech, start a movement, or shout on the street corner.

BaBy StEpS

It all starts with defining what you believe and who you are for yourself. Then you can work on speaking in a way that supports that. You've probably heard the saying about a wise person having two ears and one mouth—use them proportionally. Good advice! When in doubt, it's okay to just take a moment and listen to those around you. Anytime we talk with family and friends, we make sure that it's truly a two-way conversation. Our goal is not to be combative, but open and kind. Start with being kind to yourself. Just remember, you're a conservative, you're already one step ahead of those bozos anyway.

Arm Yourself with Facts

No matter your opinion about anything that matters to you, there is nothing wrong with it—so be proud that you're a MAGA mom! Next, be sure you know what you're talking about. Have you ever watched those street interviews where passersby are asked some question and they show how misinformed they truly are? You do *not* want to be that person. Girls, listen—start small. Watch the first fifteen minutes of Tucker Carlson and then switch it Bravo for some good trash TV. These are baby steps for a reason. We would never want you to get rid of *The Housewives*. That's just evil. Perhaps later in your life, you will slowly ease into all the life-changing information some of our favorite conservative pundits have to offer—like Dan Bongino with *The Bongino Report*, Jack Posobiec with OANN, or Sean Hannity on Fox. But for now, fifteen minutes. It will be enough to hold a conversation if you just keep up with the daily grind of what's going on in D.C. The more you know about why you support certain platforms, candidates, and policies, the more confident you will be.

Be a Good Listener

Refer back to the two ears, one mouth analogy. The best way to connect with someone is to ask them a question. People aren't so combative when you ask them to share why they think a certain way. Then, really listen. When someone else is talking, that's not the time for you to be planning what you'll say next. Every time we talk with family and friends, we ask them why they feel the way they do. We give them a chance to explain, and we just listen. Then and only then, do we lovingly share the way we see it. Do not demand that others think the same way you do.

Practice Your Responses

This may seem funny, but it's really the best way to learn how to articulate your thoughts. It's a bit like preparing for a speech or a debate. Imagine the questions you might be asked and be ready with thoughtful answers. The only way to really do this is to practice. More than once, we've been doing something like washing dishes and one of our kids asks who we're talking to. "No one, sweetie. I'm talking to an imaginary angry liberal!" No one wants to sound stupid, so prepare in advance! And trust me, just ask any of our trolls on twitter, we sound stupid all the time. If you find yourself in a situation where you feel the blood rush coming on, don't let it get you down. There's always next time. More talking to yourself while doing dishes.

BiG StEpS

Once you feel really prepared, you can venture out to have conversations. It's okay to start with people who may already agree with you. You can practice sharing ideas and asking questions with your spouse or best friend. Maybe you have a buddy who also wants to be more vocal; you can have real conversations over coffee or, if you like to live on the wild side, a couple bottles of liquid courage. For us, that is wine. And, even if you agree with someone in general, you can always learn more about their thoughts and ideas. Here are a few reminders as you venture out to speak with your crazy uncle or opinionated sister-in-law.

Find Common Ground

If you are ready for a big conversation with friends and family, it's always important to find common ground first. Please don't ever think finding your voice means fighting with people. We get enough of focusing on what makes us different, try to keep that common ground up front. Often if we agree on the big picture stuff, it's easier to have a productive, honest conversation about differing viewpoints.

Don't Take the Cheap Shot

You see this quite a bit on social media (which we'll talk about in a later chapter), but we're always amazed when people jump into a conversation with their guns blazing. This can also happen at the neighborhood picnic, or even in the church parking lot. Yes, there are those who just want to get people riled up, but don't take the bait and don't lower yourself to that level. Remember, there is anger (and dare we say fear) on both sides. If you react from that place, you may miss the opportunity to have an important conversation. When all else fails, you can throw out your version of *bless your heart!*

Ask More Questions

Yes, you have to know your facts. If you are actually getting into a political conversation, be informed, but understand that the other person may not be. You might be surprised that the majority of people get their knowledge, on any given issue, from a meme they saw on Facebook. They don't have the facts and they often don't know why they feel the way they do. Asking a few questions lets them know you're trying to hear them. Having real facts will help you ask intelligent questions, present the truth, and help you lovingly stand your ground. If it turns out those idiots don't have enough brains to saddle a June bug after you performed your big fact throwdown, just pray for them.

Comments from the Choir

We think it's really important to remember when having conversations with friends and family that disagree with us, that the probability of us changing anyone's mind is close to zero. We approach every situation to understand and hear people out. More than anything, we believe the divide in this nation needs to heal, and for that to happen, people have to be able to hear each other out. Every once in a while, you may actually be able to accomplish that and that's great. That's why there is such a strong "walk away" movement; it does happen.

Notes

Notes

Notes

CHAPTER THREE

RAISING KIDS
WHO ARE PROUD AMERICANS

"Direct your children onto the right path, and when they are older,
they will not leave it."

—PROVERBS 22:6

We love being moms and are thrilled we have been blessed with the opportunity. We believe raising children is the most important job out there, because it's today's children who will become tomorrow's leaders. No matter how much time you have, whether you're stay-at-home or you leave the house to work outside the home every day, we know every mom does the best she can. We all get some things right and some things wrong. Some days it feels like you could throw yourself on the floor and miss, right? So, please know this is not about adding to your to-do list or giving you some sage advice because we think we know better. We're in this together and, as MAGA moms, we believe part of raising our children is instilling in them your faith, your love of God and country, and, dare we say it, respect for our president.

That sounds pretty basic, but these days it can take more effort than you realize. We cannot expect the schools, their friends, or the internet to give our children the foundation we want them to have. We know that because that's our job. But added to that, is having to re-educate against some of what your kids are learning out there in the world. There is so much chatter, noise, and influence out there that strays away from traditional values (things that used to just be called values). There is too much emphasis on being rewarded just for showing up—it's no wonder so many kids feel entitled! There is also a negative trend in pop culture that sends the message that it's okay to disrespect America and that we should feel guilty about being patriots. That. Is. Crazy! Our kids need to understand that freedom of speech is not freedom from speech. We know that everyone doesn't have the same opinion, but let's be sure our children are proud to live in a country that allows all those different opinions.

In the first two chapters, we talked about ways to show and speak about your patriotism. Our hope for this chapter is that you will be able to put feet to those ideas and raise your kids to be just as proud as you are. Sharing your values and educating your kids is going to look a little different in every home and with every family. The ideas we have here are things we do or that have inspired us. Focus on what speaks to you and works for your family. Little things, big things, all things make a difference. How we act, speak, and behave at home helps demonstrate to our children how to act outside the home.

Things to Do

We are our children's role models, and we believe one of the most important things we can demonstrate is kindness. In all of the teaching, learning, speaking, doing, whether they're baby steps or big steps, everything should be done through the filter of kindness. Stand up for what we believe, but don't trample on someone else's belief in the process. As you read through these ideas and activities, remember to keep kindness in the forefront.

BaBy StEpS

Are we the only ones who struggle to get one more thing done in any given day? We're all so busy and, it seems, our kids are just as busy. It sometimes feels like a miracle just to get everyone out the door with shoes on—bonus points if they match! That's why these ideas are things you can do without planning an extra outing or event, just by adding some things to what you're already doing.

Add American History to the Reading List

Most students of reading age have a list of books they have to read throughout the school year. Some schools even have summer reading challenges. The way we see it, the kids are reading anyway, so just be sure there are some books that share the facts about our country's history. Scan the list to see if there are some great titles already included. One series we like is the *I Survived* series by Lauren Tarshis. They're told from the perspective of a child that survived a major historical event. The cool thing about these books is that it's a great way for your kids to step into someone else's shoes. If you can't find or afford these books, visit the library (which you can do online) and see what books are available for your child's reading level.

Take Advantage Being in the Car

We are pretty technology free in our house, but while we have those little boogers strapped in their seats, we like to take advantage of that time to fill those little noggins with knowledge. A lot of cars now have DVD players to entertain kids while on the road. Or other families choose to just have iPads in the car. More often than not, we all have the latest kid craze movie playing, right? How about some of the time, you play a DVD that tells a story from history. We're not pushing anyone to buy anything, but one of the resources we have found useful is the *Learn Our History* series, cofounded by Mike Huckabee. These DVDs offer a fun way for kids to learn American history, and using them in the car promises a captive audience! Again, explore your local library for resources and videos you can check out without breaking your budget.

Map Out Your Next Road Trip

Whether you're driving across the country, across the state, or even across town, chances are there are some historical sites along the way. Do a little research before your next trip and plan to stop at some of these sites to give your kids an in-person glace at history. Depending on where you live, you should be able to share some of the cultural diversity that makes up our great country. Even if you don't have a big trip planned, maybe you can take your children to a veteran's memorial cemetery. They can see how many people have given their lives to provide them the freedoms they enjoy every day. If you can, schedule these visits around planned stops so you're saving a bit of time and making more of each meal on the road. We took our kids to the veteran's memorial in Houston and also did the wreath-laying ceremony at Arlington Cemetery. It was such an incredible experience, and I know those memories will always stick with them.

Fly and Fold Your Flag

We know we talked about flying your flag in an earlier chapter. We hope you're doing that, but a great way to take this a step further is to be sure your kids are involved. Have them raise the flag when you put it out. Teach them how to properly fold and store the flag when you bring it inside. Here's a great website that shows you how to do just that: https://www.usflag.org/fold.flag.html. Even if you already know all of this, it's a great activity for your kids to look this up and learn. Also, share the versions of our flag through history so they truly understand what each star and stripe really mean to our freedom.

BiG StEpS

When you have a bit more time, you can take on some bigger projects. Maybe plan something for over a weekend, holiday, or summer break when you aren't shuffling kids back and forth between school and extracurricular activities. These are some of the things we have done over the years, and we found that once we started doing some of these things, they got easier to accomplish. Also, remember to call reinforcements. Get together with other MAGA moms and work on some of these things together. Not only will you get to share the workload, but you'll be able to have some time with like-minded friends in the process.

The Old-Fashioned Lemonade Stand

Okay, your kids don't have to sell lemonade, but this activity is about the lesson of earning reward and the value of hard work. If a lemonade stand doesn't work for you because you live in an apartment, maybe your kids could walk the neighbor's dog, mow someone's grass, or run an errand here or there. We, personally, send our kids out to be neighborhood poop patrol, where we make them pick up all the dog poop people may have left behind. They absolutely detest us for this, but I'm sure it is something they will even make their own children do to learn the value of hard work. Besides, it brings a little sick joy to us to watch them take on a task we have detested for years. Bottom line: you want to teach your children the value of earning their own money and the satisfaction of accomplishing something on their own. The biggest challenge on this one may be not being that "helicopter mom" and letting your kids figure things out on their own. Give them guidance, answer questions, help them with the setup, and do ask them questions about how things are going and what they're learning. Bonus points if they can earn money toward something they want!

Baking Cookies for Others

What's better than the smell of your favorite cookie baking in the oven? Not much. But why not bake some cookies for someone else? This is a great way to teach your kids about reaching out and being kind to others. A giving spirit is developed by what you teach them through example. This can be as easy as baking a batch of chocolate chip cookies for your elderly neighbor, but we also like to include our first responders. While you're mixing and baking, explain to your children what firefighters and police officers do for your community. When they're ready, all you have to do is drop them off at the fire or police station—no question they'll be appreciated. No big fanfare or advance planning is needed as they're open 24/7, so it can fit into your schedule. More bonus points—have your kids write a thank-you note. By the way, delivering cookies and such is just fine in our area. However, before you do this in your hometown, contact your local police or fire department to confirm what they are allowed to accept. Believe it or not, some stations cannot accept homemade goodies because of the risk of someone using that gesture to actually harm first responders with poison. If homemade baked goods are out of the question, chances are they can accept pizza delivery or gift cards from a local restaurant. This activity is really about the gesture, not the actual treat, so find out what would make them feel appreciated and do that!

Have Your Kids Host a Patriotic Party

This one will take a bit more planning and is an ideal opportunity to join forces with your friends or neighbors. The trick here is for you to do as little of the planning as possible so your children can step up and show their patriotism in their own way. Pick a holiday that works in your schedule—it could be the traditional 4th of July or Memorial Day, but what about a Flag Day or Veterans Day party? Let the kids plan the menu, activities, and decorations. You can set a budget and take them shopping with you to gather the supplies. Let them search the internet for some patriotic music or party games. It can be as big or small as you want (and can afford), because the real focus of this one is having your children put their patriotism on parade! By the way, this is an easy potluck event, so you don't have to worry about feeding a crowd. Major bonus points if you can get this to count for some kind of extra credit with your kids' schools!

Comments from the Choir

We're quite sure that everyone has their favorite cookie recipe, but we wanted to share one of our favorites with you. This recipe is *super* easy and is the one we use when we're baking cookies for our local first responders and pretty much any event or holiday. As over the top as it sounds, we always do this recipe one batch regular and one batch with the cup for cup gluten-free flour blend. It may seem like a little much, but when it comes to our first responders, we always want to make sure no one is left out because of a gluten allergy. Besides, we've realized it doesn't affect the taste or texture at all.

Oatmeal Lace Cookies

Ingredients:

    1 egg, room temperature and lightly beaten

    2 ¼ cups quick oats

    3 tbsp all-purpose flour

    2 ¼ cups brown sugar, lightly packed

    1 tsp salt

    1 tsp vanilla

    2 sticks (1 cup) unsalted butter

1. Preheat oven to 375° Fahrenheit (190° Celsius).

2. Line baking sheets with silicone baking mats or parchment paper. Set aside.

3. Heat butter and brown sugar in a large saucepan over medium heat, stirring frequently until butter has melted and mixture is smooth.

4. Stir in salt, flour, and oats, and carefully mix until the oats are fully covered with the brown sugar/butter mixture.

5. Add the lightly beaten egg and vanilla extract. Stir until fully incorporated.

6. Drop cookie batter by the teaspoon onto prepared baking sheets, leaving at least 2 inches between each cookie to allow them to spread.

7. Bake for 5 minutes, until the edges are golden brown. Keep a close eye on these, as the bake time can vary based on how much batter you use for each cookie.

8. Allow to cool on the cookie sheet for 5 minutes, then move to wire racks to cool completely.

9. If you don't plan to eat them immediately, store in an airtight container. They last for up to 7 days.

Notes

Notes

Notes

Notes

YOUR COMMUNITY

CHAPTER FOUR

JUST SHOWING UP: THE BEST START

"Action indeed is the sole medium of expression for ethics."

—JANE ADDAMS

Creating a patriotic home life is a foundation that you can build on to have a bigger impact. From there, it is just a small step to sharing your voice, your heart, your faith, and your patriotism with your community. For us, one of the most important ways we do this is to practice kindness to those around us. If we cannot be kind to others, how can we expect them to ever listen to our point of view? Of course, we should be kind to everyone, but to make a difference, we really need to practice being kind to those who think differently than us. Luke 6:33 says, "And if you do good only to those who do good to you, why should you get credit? Even sinners do the same." We have to reach out to others. We don't want folks to have a preconceived notion about who we are because of how we vote. That means that we have to reciprocate, right? The wonderful thing about kindness is that it doesn't take any money and usually not a lot of extra time. Being kind is really about just showing up and being present in each moment; it can be that simple. That's why it's the best start to reaching out to your community.

45

Imagine if everyone would just focus on being truly kind to those in their house and their surrounding neighbors; what a different world we would have. Being kind is more than not being mean: it's about being actively caring and considerate. In today's divisive world, I think we can all agree that more kindness is a good thing. Too many people are looking for what divides us and have a bias about how "other people" are. As MAGA moms, we get that. In the news and across social media, we hear negative messages about how Trump supporters and conservatives are hateful, homophobic, racist people. That hurts because it's not true and it's judging us without knowing us. Instead of arguing back, we've found it better to just be kind. Why? Because actions will speak louder than any words we can say. And, honestly, sometimes we're still unsure of what to say in defense of who we really are, we can get all tongue-tied and defensive. Guess what? Being kind to others takes no prep work and no special words! Not long ago, we were walking around New York City in our MAGA hats. You'd be surprised that we mostly received high-fives and "cool hat" comments, but a few times we got "the bird," by a combative individual, and we would just smile and wave. Sometimes if were feeling snarky, a simple, "Ah, do you need a hug?" slips out, but hey, that's still kind, right?

Here's an obvious point—if you don't show up anywhere, you'll never have the chance to demonstrate your kindness. We have to first show up and connect with others before we can hope to make a difference. Getting involved can feel overwhelming because who has more time and energy? You also might be a little worried that if you show up somewhere, you may end up on some committee doing something you care about but don't have time to manage. There is an easy way to be sure this doesn't happen. Practice using the word *no*! Yes, this book is about you getting courageous and sharing your patriotism with others, but it's not about you taking on more than you can handle. So, start small by showing up and standing firm in what works for you and your family. When it's time, we hope you'll get more involved, but when and how much is up to you! Guilt-free zone!

Things to Do

In case you haven't figured it out yet, each chapter pushes you a bit more out of your comfort zone. Proceed at your own comfort level, but be ready to step up to the next stage when it's time. The first three chapters are about doing this within the safety of your own home, hence the section title, "Your Home"! At this point, it's time to reach out a bit into your own community and show your patriotic heart to others. Now, slap on that MAGA hat and let's get to it!

BaBy StEpS

We like having these little baby steps that can easily be added on to whatever you're already doing or don't take a lot of time and money. These ideas are about being intentional in what we say and do. Be present. Put down your phone and look up at the person you're interacting with, right? Don't get us wrong, we love our cell phones and they do make life much easier. Still, they don't replace the chance to connect with someone and help them in ways you didn't even know they needed.

Smile at Others

This is one of those simple things that gets easily lost in the crazy of each day. We're often so busy thinking about what our next to-do is that we're barely aware of the current thing we're doing. A great example is shopping. You've got to run by the grocery store after picking up the kids to get whatever. Then it's home to the list of things waiting for you there. You're more than distracted and, when it's us, we're usually tired and hungry. Practice this once you're in line to pay. Put your phone away. We saw a woman in front of us on the phone the entire time she was checking out, ignoring everyone. We get it, we're all busy. Communicating with the person bagging your groceries may seem like a waste of time, but that is a great opportunity to just connect with a stranger and share kindness!

We're sure she was really busy, but it seemed rude and we noticed the checker's head was down. So, please put away the phone. Take a deep breath. Look up at the checker and smile! They may be shocked, but they'll smile back. Ask them how their day is going and really listen to the answer. You may be the only genuine interaction they get all day! Be present and make small moments count. Also, you are teaching your kids to be in the moment and aware of those around them. Because we tend to shop at the same store and the same times, we often see the same workers. How great to know them well enough to call them by name, ask how their vacation was, or whatever. This doesn't take extra time, but it can turn their day around. It will likely lift your mood, as well.

Use a Prayer List

How many times have you seen someone post on social media "Praying for you" or "Saying Prayers" or "Sending love"? Do you think they really stop to pray or just type words and move on? We're not pointing any fingers because we've done it too—that's how we know sometimes that's all that happens. So, if you say you're going to pray, do it right then! If you can't, have a place where you write down who you're praying for and why. Another thing we like to do is be very specific in how we're praying for that person. It's a simple way to show them we heard their request and are showing up in their world to support them. If possible, check back with them to see how things are going.

Attend the Holiday Bazaar

Maybe it's the holiday bazaar or maybe it's the local farmer's market, the VFWs (Veterans of Foreign Wars) pancake breakfast, or some other local event. One of the best ways you can show up in your community is to literally show up! Events can only be successful if people attend, so be one of those people. If you're pressed for time or money, select those that don't have a cost and walk through the doors. It's not an all-day obligation; just an hour or so can make a difference. Talk with a few vendors and meet some new people. The great thing is if you do this often, you'll see some familiar faces. They'll appreciate that you showed up and stopped to check in with them. Sure, if budget allows, buy a little something. But we want you to focus on the showing up—that's the vital first step.

Share a Post

Speaking of local events, very often our favorite community causes and organizations have social media pages where they post information about those events, fundraisers, and goals. We see them and often, like we do with most every other post, we scroll right past it. We may hit a *like* or *interested* button. We may plan to go or know we can't attend, but regardless, there's still a way for you to "show up" online. Share that post and let your social media community know about this event and that it's important to you. Even if it's something you can't participate in, you may encourage someone else to go.

BiG StEpS

These ideas will take more time and require some effort, but the impact will likely match your efforts. As you work on making real connections within your community, you'll find that the positive reactions will inspire you to do more. We encourage you to involve your children with these things as much as possible, so they learn how to support their community as well.

Share the Sweets

How often do your kids come home from their evening of Halloween trick or treating and have more candy than they need? We're not talking about a few extra pieces of chocolate; we're talking about mountains of sweets that, if consumed, will definitely lead your kids into a sugar high that will send you up a wall or your kids straight to the dentist with cavities. Since there can be too much of a good thing, we have our kids share their Halloween candy. It's not really about too much candy, but we use it as a way to support the military. We box it up and send it to soldiers overseas. In some ways, that may seem like a small thing, but it is a valuable teaching moment to help your kids think about others. Explain to them that soldiers are serving our country and don't get Halloween. It's a little freedom we have that we don't want to take for granted. We recommend letting your children pick their favorites to keep and enjoy or you may end up with anarchy on your hands. Depending on the age of your children, they may not understand and give you some pushback—or a temper tantrum—but what better way to teach about sacrifice than asking a child to give up some of their hard-won candy? You may want to give them a prize of some sort if they do this. We've actually done that.

Don't you go judging us now; this is a process, people! You're letting our military know they're remembered *and* you're teaching your kids about giving back. If they aren't on board initially, they are learning, and we promise their hearts will eventually catch up. Did we mention this was a process? By the way, you can check online for the best way to do this in our community. Here's a great website to get started: https://www.operationgratitude.com/express-your-thanks/halloween-candy/

Visit the Senior Center

This is a great thing to do any time, but especially during the holidays, when seniors often feel lonely, or even forgotten. Whether family can't (or won't) visit or they have no family left, a visit from someone who cares will change their lives, if only for a day. It's a good idea to check with the senior center or housing facility you have in mind to visit. You will need to confirm when is the best time to visit and any guidelines they have in place. They may even be hosting a holiday party that would be an ideal event where you and your kids can bring some extra joy. You can share treats, sing songs, or just spend some time getting to know these precious neighbors. Again, checking with the facility beforehand will help you prepare and bring what they most need. Just being there is the most important thing, so don't worry too much about anything else.

Throw an Appreciation Party

This idea is a step beyond taking cookies to first responders. We think it's important to really let them know how appreciated they are, and throwing a party is a great way to do just that. After several officer killings a couple years ago, we knew we needed to lift up the spirits of the people who keep our community safe. It may sound like a lot of work, but all we did was post some flyers in our area's businesses and make a few posts on our social media pages to explain our plan. We had people all around the area stepping up to send donations, offer catering, and provide raffle items and gift basket goodies. It became a great way to connect with our community. Start with confirming the date and location—your church or community hall may be a great option to host, and some stations have community rooms that can be used for this. Then, invite your firefighters and/or police officers to their own appreciate day party. It can be as simple as cake and ice cream, so don't be too concerned with the details. It's about the doing. Ours was a great success and our kids (who dressed up as officers) really enjoyed getting to meet the police and better understand what they do for us every day—and they got to check out their patrol cars! It was a huge payoff and our officers really appreciated it.

Comments from the Choir

Confession time! This is Cjaye and I just wanted to share a story to hopefully take some pressure off some of the moms reading this. We've been going to visit the senior center for years, but it didn't always go smoothly. When my kids were very little, my daughter was really scared. She was so overwhelmed and frightened that she would hide behind my legs when I was introducing her to any of the residents. I would gently push her out from under my legs and have her talk to the person and give them a hug. It was a struggle and I wondered if it was worth it. Well? Fast-forward a few years and now when we visit, she runs inside and hugs *everyone*! She gives them candy, listens to them, and even sings for them. It's adorable and it makes us all happy. But, please note, she wasn't born that way. It was taught. It was repeatedly going there to visit and cultivating her heart towards kindness to them that eventually stuck with her. Relax if your children don't do these things eagerly, and certainly not on their own. We are teaching our children through repetitive acts of kindness, and that compassion does eventually get written on their hearts! Stick with it!

Notes

Notes

Notes

Notes

CHAPTER FIVE

TAKING A STAND AND MAKING A DIFFERENCE

"So then, dear brothers and sisters, be firm.
Do not be moved! Always be outstanding in the work of the Lord,
knowing that your labor is not in vain in the Lord."

—1 CORINTHIANS 15:58

As you get to know you community better, you'll begin to see where you can make a difference. Where you can stand together with other MAGA moms or organizations that need strength in numbers. What are the local issues in your community that need your patriotic support? It doesn't have to be the biggest and most publicized event or cause. In fact, sometimes it's the smaller programs that will benefit the most from you taking a stand alongside them. If you really want to make that difference, it's not a bad idea to think beyond the most well-known programs that have the most PR supporting them. What if there's a smaller group that is just getting started, but what they're doing is so very important? Spend some time thinking about what community issues and causes matter to you and your family. Perhaps you have a program at your church or school that speaks to your heart. That's where you should start focusing your time and talents. And, if you want to have your family involved, get them into the process of selecting the charities, organizations, or causes that mean the most to you as a family.

Do a little online research and create a list of things happening in your community. Take a look at their websites and social media pages to see what they have going and if there's an easy way for you to plug into their efforts. Make a list if you want to share this with your family and you can all work together to decide why you want to support these different causes and how you might do that. Once you pick an organization or group, reach out to them and let them know they've got themselves some new groupies! Trust us, you might think they have it all under control and your help isn't needed, but put away those negative voices; pretty much any group you want to help will appreciate you reaching out. They also likely have a list of immediate needs, so you won't have to figure out how to best help them; they'll already know! What we want this effort to be about is working to make your community better—any part of your community. Bottom line: you don't have to change the world to change the world in which you live.

Once you've figured out the best cause or organization for you to stand alongside, it's time to determine at what capacity you can be involved. It's easy to get caught up in the excitement of something new, and it's easy to think you're a superwoman—because let's be honest, you are awesome! We just don't want you feeling busier than a three-legged cat in a litter box, so don't bite off more than you can chew, girl. Be sure it fits with your schedule and you're not promising something you are unable to deliver. We don't want our fellow MAGA moms to suffer from burnout or set themselves up for failure. That being said, it's also okay to challenge yourself to do something you haven't done before—if you're anything like us, you'll be leaping before you look and singing in front of sixty thousand people at a Trump rally when you haven't even been on a stage before, so please, look before you leap. Do as we say, not as we do!

Things to Do

When it comes to making a stand, it doesn't always have to be a physical activity, but it will require you take some action, give of your time and sometimes, you'll have to put your money where your mouth is. We've got some great ideas for you to look over to see what best fits your style. We're going to share some specific causes that mean a lot to us, but we are in no way telling you what causes to support. We just want to be honest about our hearts and hope it will inspire you to do the same.

BaBy StEpS

These baby steps are things that can pretty much be done in the comfort of your own home. Often, when you have a cause or organization you're going to focus on, you'll support them in various ways. You may find some of these suggestions are things you can do for the same group. There's nothing wrong with that. You can spread your love and support around to a variety of groups or heap the majority of your attention onto one cause. There is no wrong way to stand with a charity or effort that matters to you.

Fill the Donation Envelope

Most donations can now be made online through a website or funding site. Charities are great at making it easy for you to give money, so it will be painless. Chances are, you already have a group in mind that you've thought about funding in the past. This can be a low-key way to begin to work with an organization and make sure your money is spent the way you hope. The great thing about local groups is they typically have fewer overheads, so a greater portion of your donation goes to the actual program and services they represent. We're not saying anything negative about national and international charities, but it's obvious that the fewer staff and fewer administrative needs, the more that's available to go direct to those in need. We support a local pregnancy center because the pro-life stance is very important to us. Places like this are forgotten and many people don't even know they exist. They're small and local, but they provide resources for scared, vulnerable women who might be contemplating an abortion. Our center also helps them out with delivery needs and has resources to help raise the baby.

Join the Organization

If the cause you're supporting is membership driven, has a board of directors or otherwise needs people to be on a roster, take that step. Yes, that means putting your name down in writing, possibly paying dues, and attending meetings on a regular basis. Do it! There is strength in numbers, and we all need to know we're not in this on our own. The cool thing is you're going to meet some like-minded people and have a new set of friends. We understand this is a step that, while easy, does take some time, so only do this if you can be an effective member. Maybe it's just joining and attending an annual gala or event. Maybe the ask is for a monthly or quarterly meeting. Check out the expectations—they usually have them on their website—and if it is indeed a fit, sign on the dotted line!

Shop Local

For us, this is a no-brainer, but we want to be clear that we still shop at Costco and other chain stores and do more than our fair share of shopping via Amazon. However, we like to make a point to support our local businesses, especially those belonging to other patriotic community members. We're not fans of the cancel culture and boycotting this or that. Instead, we focus on patronizing shops and using the services of those who share our love of God and country. An easy place to start is if your church has a bulletin board where members can post their flyers and business cards. If you need to get your gutters cleaned, why not try a company whose owner attends your church? Remember the suggestion in the previous chapter to attend the holiday bazaar or local farmer's market? That's another place to easily spend a little money to support your neighborhood businesses. When you stand with a small, local business, you're doing more than just making a sale. You're helping that person put food on their table and send their kids to sports camp. Every sale matters!

BiG StEpS

Alright y'all, you ready to jump in with both feet yet? These ideas will have you diving a little deeper, spending a little more time, and having some real accountability. It can certainly be easier to do things we can fit into our schedule and do on our own time, but when you're ready to really make a difference, adjusting your schedule won't be as impossible as you think. We all make time for things that matter, especially when those things allow us to share our faith and patriotism.

Mail the Letters

Mail the letters, make the calls, or send the emails. Most charitable organizations need help getting their message out there, and this may be just the thing for you. They should have the contact list for you, and even the template email or letter (or phone script). All you have to do is stand up to help them get the word out for their annual fundraiser, next event, or current needs list. Although this is often something you can do at home, we have this as a big step because this group is relying on you to accomplish the task. There's nothing worse than dropping the ball, so be sure you have all the details, including if there's a deadline. Then, start reaching out to share the news.

Volunteer for the Event

Nearly every charitable organization has an annual event. They range from fancy galas, to silent auctions, to picnics, to fun runs. These events cannot happen without help from volunteers. Find an event for an organization that speaks to your heart. Maybe it's something for veterans, or single moms, or homeless teens. Whatever it is, step up to decorate the venue, fill a table, gather auction items, or even clean up after it's over. One that we really believe in is an organization called 40 Days for Life (www.40daysforlife.com) that is pro-life like we are. They coordinate a focused, forty-day, nonstop, round-the-clock prayer vigil outside a single Planned Parenthood center or other abortion facility in your community. They create this as a peaceful and educational presence. Those who are called to stand witness during this twenty-four-hour-a-day presence send a powerful message to the community about the tragic reality of abortion. It really makes a difference and women have changed their mind about their abortions. They have all the details, so you don't have to reinvent the wheel; they just need volunteers to help make it happen. If this type of event speaks to you, check out their website. Don't worry, you don't have to be on-site for all forty days, but maybe you could help fill the schedule.

Organize the Food/Clothing Drive

Chances are good that you already know an organization that operates a food bank or clothing closet. Reach out to them and offer to organize or head up the next drive. If they don't have something organized, you can do this yourself. Don't panic; it's not as hard as you might think at first. Simply reach out to the neighborhood and let them know you're collecting. Ask local businesses if they'll take a barrel or box so their employees and customers can drop off the needed items. You can have a set time frame for this one (it doesn't last forever). When it's over, you pick them up—or arrange pickup—and deliver them to the facility. Yes, you will need to confirm the guidelines for donations; the organization may have a most-needed items list you can share. This is a great event to start online and use the power of social media to spread the word, get volunteers, and gather donations.

Comments from the Choir

This is Lyndsey, and if you read my bio, you probably know already why the pro-life message is so important to me. One of my sweet babies has Kabuki Syndrome. It's a genetic disorder that brings some amazing challenges with it, but I wouldn't change one thing about my child. That's why it rips my heart apart when I think of all the babies that are aborted because they discovered the child has a "defect." Gosh, they don't even know what a wonderful world they are missing!

Even after Joey was born, people questioned her worth! Her heart surgeon told me I didn't have to give her life-saving heart surgery if I didn't want to. He said I didn't have to be a hero and I could choose not to repair her heart and let her die of natural causes. Y'all, this still stabs me in the heart. What if I had listened to him? Oh, my how my life would be so different. She brings *so much* joy to me and everyone she meets. She has taught me more about love and acceptance in her few years with me than I ever learned before she came. She is *the* reason I fight for the voiceless. These special needs kids and adults are gifts and it is a damn tragedy that people see otherwise. We must change this. All of these babies are just as human as me and you, and they all deserve the right to life.

I look at my precious Joey Belle and see all the joy she has and love she gives. I know she is just as deserving of life as anyone else! In fact, we have a song, "Made to Love You," written from an unborn baby's perspective to help share the message that every life is a special gift. I share this with you so you understand why the pro-life movement is so important to us and, I hope you'll find a cause or issue you can be as passionate about.

Notes

Notes

Notes

CHAPTER SIX

MAKING LOCAL MATTERS MATTER

"Always vote for principle, though you may vote alone, and you may cherish the sweetest reflection that your vote is never lost."

—JOHN QUINCY ADAMS

"All politics is local." That quote has been credited to former speaker of the House Tip O'Neill, and on many levels it still rings true. We get it that there is now a twenty-four-hour news feed and social media available at a flick of our fingers. With that national and international politics show up in our households every day. Sometimes it's easy to get caught up in what's going on in Washington, D.C. or Europe—and we do need to pay attention to and be aware of what's going on in the world. However, with all that national news focus, we have to keep in mind that news shows are part news and part entertainment. Honestly, if you're a reality TV fan, turn on the news; it's the best reality television. What they make a big deal of and cover 24/7 is about winning the ratings game, and unfortunately, much of the news we receive is not very objective. So pay attention for sure, but it's important to remember that what happens in our own city hall matters and impacts us more directly. Of course, it's more than just city hall—it can also be your local PTA, school board, or even an area business association that deserved our attention. Things are happening locally, and if you don't get involved you have no say. So, we might adjust that quote to say, "All local matters matter!" If you're a MAGA mom with a patriotic spirit, we know there are community issues that are important to you and your family and will impact your daily life. It's important to tune into those and be sure your voice is heard!

You won't have to look very hard to find the trouble spots. Is there a homeless issue in your town? Do your local veterans have what they need? Are there city and county taxes, levies, and legislation that are getting out of control? Watch the local news and read the local paper, or check out your city's Facebook page. A lot happens on our own city streets, and as true patriots, we need to find ways to speak out about what we feel about it. Remember, we share all this with a large dose of reality. We don't expect you to fight city hall or run for public office—unless, of course, you want to. What you can do is share your passion. Bring your MAGA mom voice to the meeting and share your perspective. It's easy to think you don't need to get involved because someone else is going to do that, but as the saying goes, "There was an important job to be done and Everyone was sure that Someone would do it. Anyone could have done it, but No one did it." It's time for us to be the Someone who did something.

Where is it you most feel patriots like you are being underrepresented? What is one of the best local issues a God-loving, proud American like you should support? What can you do to help create the kind of community you want to live in and raise your family? It's easy to feel that as one person, one voice, there's not a lot you can do. But most movements start with one person saying *enough*! Maybe you need to offer that different perspective or ask that tough question. The next time you hear or read about a local issue and it pushes your buttons and makes you think something should be done, ask yourself if it's time for you to do something. Besides, mothers are often the ones to step in and get things done. We didn't pay a lot of attention to the world around us until we became moms. Now, as we see our kid's futures crumbling, we are driven to step into the boxing ring and kick some political butt!

Things to Do

The great thing about getting involved in local issues is that most of the time, the structure already exists. You are not going to have to figure out what to do or how to get involved—you'll just tap into your issue or cause and there will be a way for you to make a stand and share your input. How much time you give to any give cause is, of course, up to you and what you can do without making yourself crazy. We believe family comes first, but we balance that out with knowing when giving some time to something will help our families in the long run. The ideas we share here require varying levels of involvement, so trust your gut! The biggest hurdle for you might be being brave enough to share your opinion with others.

BaBy StEpS

Some of the easy, little things we can do are things we're hopefully already doing. Still, we know that life can get busy and things we mean to do don't get done. Heck, that's one of us pretty much every day! Just being sure to pick up the kids from school on time, and heck, getting them there in the first place, are major accomplishments. As with all our ideas, this is about finding what works for you.

Show Up and Vote

Americans have been given some amazing rights as citizens, and voting has to be one of the greatest! Many elections now offer mail-in ballots, so you don't even have to take the time to go by the polling place: you just vote your conscience and drop your ballot in the mail! However, if you've never taken your kids out to see an in-person polling location, we highly recommend it. There's something about showing up and seeing those voting machines that makes you grateful that we have a voice and open elections. And it can be a great opportunity to explain the privilege of voting to your kids. Plus, the kids love wearing your "I voted" sticker. Remember to vote in *every* election! Most of us vote every four years in the presidential election, but have you ever seen the stats on voter turnout for local elections? It's appalling that so few citizens vote at these times. That means that a small percentage of your community is deciding things for you. Please, never miss an opportunity to vote!

Show Up at the Meeting

Nearly every issue is brought up in a public meeting. From city councils to PTAs, there are regular meetings—and sometimes special meetings—to discuss what's going on in your community. Sometimes there are mailers notifying you about a public information meeting, but regardless, you can do a little online research to find when and where these meetings are being held. Make a note, put it in your schedule, and show up. Even if you just sit in the back of the room and hear what others are saying, that's more than most people do. You'll be better informed and can then decide to get more involved—or not. If you feel strongly about an issue, it's okay to be one of those people that steps up to the mic. You can prepare a few thoughts or ask a question. When you do decide to speak up, remember to do so in kindness. No one likes to listen to someone yell, but you can voice your opinion clearly and without being aggressive. We also get that there are times when you may be angry—been there, girl. Been there.

Spread the Word

It's surprising the number of people who are truly not informed about the world around them. It is likely a combination of misinformation, misunderstanding, and sadly, apathy. One of the things you can do without judging anyone is just share what you've learned. If you attended a meeting and learned new facts, that's a great thing to share. Get on your social media account and let folks know—it's a simple as that. Something like, "I went to the XYZ meeting last night and one of the things on the agenda was Issue ABC. Did you know that [fill in fact or data here]?" Also, this makes you look super smart to the jerks from high school that called you a space cadet. This is just a general assessment. Nothing personal here.

That's really all you have to do. You know what social media is like and you *know* you're going to get people liking your post, sharing your post, and offering up their opinion. If you're worried about things getting negative, remember that it's *your* page. You can let people know you're just sharing some facts; you can be open (and should be open) to other viewpoints. Occasionally, things can get out of hand and people can become uncivil. We choose not to delete these posts and consider it good entertainment, but if it makes you uncomfortable, feel free to let people know you have the right to delete their posts if they don't behave in a manner you approve of. Another way to spread the word is to just share the announcement about a meeting that is happening. Let folks know that you'll be there and that you'd love to see them!

BiG StEpS

When you're ready to really get involved, there are always opportunities out there. Even local political candidates would love to have volunteers supporting their campaign efforts. Beyond candidates, there are often local initiatives that need to gather signatures to get on the ballot—and regardless of the side you're on, the chance to vote on something is never a bad idea. Even if your cause or issue isn't a voting one, there are ways you can give of your time to make something happen.

Coordinate a Fundraiser

We have talked a lot about political issues in this chapter, but we want to be sure you know that you don't have to dive into politics to make a difference in your community. Maybe that organization you joined needs to coordinate a big fundraiser and they just don't have the staff to make it happen. Is that a place where you can step up? Is there something that you and your kids are concerned about within the local school district? We had a friend that made it her mission to create a fundraiser for her son's high school wrestling team because they didn't have the money for new mats. That may seem small, but if your child is involved with sports, you know that kids learn valuable life lessons in accountability, commitment, and sportsmanship. That makes new wrestling mats a local issue that matters to your family. You get the idea, right? Do you and focus on what matters to you.

Volunteer for a Cause

We've touched on this idea in smaller ways, but maybe it's time for you to really step up and get involved. This is more than just joining an organization and attending an annual event. What we're talking about here is getting out into your community and getting others involved. Have you ever been approached by someone at the grocery store who's collecting signatures for something? Granted, we often blow them off because we've got shopping to do, but maybe that is a place where you can serve. Some of those issues may matter to you. Around the holidays, you see the people ringing the bell to collect donations for the Salvation Army. That can be a great place to step up and volunteer, and the Salvation Army is only one organization. Do you have a more local program that you'd like to support? Sometimes volunteering can mean manning the phones or helping with some paperwork or other administrative thing that has to happen. Local causes have limited funds and can't always hire a staff. Do you have a few hours a week to help?

Help Others Vote

One of the biggest ways we can support our president and be sure our values are represented in the House and Senate is to be sure our candidates get elected! It's vital that people get out and exercise their power to vote. You might be surprised at the number of people who aren't even registered. Scott Presler (https://scottpresler.org/), whom we mentioned earlier in the book, offers a number of great ideas on how to do this. He goes around the country and teaches people how to register. It's not hard, but too many people don't make the effort—even among Christians, who are often Republican supporters. At our church, during the midterms, our pastor allowed a nonpartisan voting registration sign-up right outside the church doors where we all walked out. That might be a great way for you to help get people registered. Talk with your pastor to see if your church can do this. You might be shocked to see the people who will line up and sign up.

Comments from the Choir

We wanted to share with you some other ideas we received from Scott Presler about helping people register to vote. It is important that you do this as a nonpartisan effort. So, obviously you can't ask if they are Republican or Democrat, but there are some nonpartisan conversation starters you can use to wave people over to the voting booth. Maybe you ask something like, "How do you feel about the wall?" Don't spend time debating with people that don't agree with you; that's rarely been effective in changing anyone's mind. Focus on the people who do, and those you can register to vote. When you aren't out registering people, you can go back to those naysayers and work on them. They may just come around if you approach them with kindness and facts.

Notes

Notes

Notes

YOUR COUNTRY

CHAPTER SEVEN

NAVIGATING PATRIOTISM ON SOCIAL MEDIA

"We are more alike, my friends, than we are unalike."

—MAYA ANGELOU

It seems like we've never in the history of the modern world been angrier and more divided than we are right now, and it shows up on our social media feeds every day. Arguments are the norm, and people are unfriended and berated at an alarming rate. What we should say is that *we* are unfriended at an alarming rate. *We* are pretty controversial, and some people can't handle it, but like we said before, we can only control ourselves and our own behavior. More on that later. Does it feel like you have to hide more and more posts, or use the "Snooze for thirty days" option for half of your friends? Do you try to avoid social media altogether? We understand if it feels that way, but does that mean you should stay quiet and never voice your opinion? Is there really only one extreme or the other? We don't believe it has to be like that, even though sometimes we choose the extreme. There is, in fact, a middle ground. There is a compassionate way to share your patriotic voice and defend

God and country without drawing blood. Everyone deserves their own voice, and although it may not feel like it in some places, we still have free speech. And dammit, we will defend it.

Social media is one of the best places for MAGA mom voices to be heard! We've talked about how you can use the power of social media to spread the word, support causes and local business, and even coordinate donations. Everything has two sides, and social media has its dark side as well. Maybe it's the anonymity that causes people to say things they wouldn't otherwise say. We call these people, "trolls in their grandma's basement." Take what they say with a grain of salt then move on. There's a sense of safety behind a computer screen because people cannot see you. Some of these people say hurtful things; remember these people are *losers*! We're bigger than that. There's also the gullibility factor. People don't really think about things before sharing with the world. They just assume it's true—especially if it backs up their own perspective. Facts be damned! It reminds us a little bit of those old-school chain letters. Do you remember those? You'd get some crazy letter that said if you didn't send copies of the letter to seven other people, you would have horrible luck and bad things would happen. Most of us knew it was a lie, but for some reason a part of us believed it or worried that it might be true. You better believe we forwarded on that chain letter! God forbid it was right and we would be broke and friendless if we didn't send it to seven people! Anyway, Facebook and other social media can spread misinformation like the online version of a bad chain letter. The worst part about this is, more often than not, this is fueled by the mainstream media. They want Trump out of office and will pretty much say anything without checking accuracy. Journalism is all but dead and it has trickled down our news feeds.

We don't want you to feel this negativity and stop using social media—no! We want you to be more active on it! We do know that as you start to share your true self, your patriotic self, there is some fear of negative reaction. Although you cannot control other people, you can always control how you react. If we remembered that there were people on the other side of every post, we would—hopefully—be more cautious and careful as we scrolled, liked, commented and shared. Our words posted on social media can reach around the globe, and that makes it a wonderful place to share the message of positive patriotism. So let's get to sharing!

Things to Do

Most of the ideas we're sharing here are about taking a moment before you do anything. Being more intentional in our online activity and in how we say what we say can go a long way in maintaining civil discourse. We've made most of the mistakes and regretted things the moment *after* we submitted a post, which is why we have a few tips to share with you.

BaBy StEpS

These ideas are really no-brainers, but when we get in a hurry or caught going down an online rabbit hole, we forget. Hopefully, these reminders will help you be more thoughtful before you have automatic reactions.

Don't Let Losers Bring You Down

Once you find your voice online, you can be sure you will be swarmed with trolls trying to make you second-guess yourself and your opinion. This is just what they do. This is cancel culture. Their main objective is to intimidate you! Don't let them succeed! Once you realize that is why they exist, it is easier to ignore them. Gosh, if we listened to half of the trolls and the negativity they spew at us, we would definitely not be here writing this book for you! Here are a few of our favorite insults we have received from some of our "fans":

- What in the country bumpkin, unseasoned chicken, cousin-lovin' Trump country is this?
- Look at those white girls, no rhythm, no upper lip.
- Yup, I'll never get that minute of my life back again.
- My ears are bleeding.
- Could y'all at least be cute if you're going to embarrass yourself like this?
- Imagine recording this and thinking it was a good idea?

That's all for now. You get the point.

Learn to Laugh

If being online doesn't bring you joy, then why are we here? If you truly believe something in your heart but don't like the reaction you are receiving, just learn to laugh it off. When we scroll through comments of people making fun of us, we truly find it entertaining and we can now laugh at ourselves. We like to say, "Life is too short to take yourself so seriously."

Do No Harm

We like to have fun, but only at our expense—never at others'. We realize in this political environment there will be a lot of hate spewed, but we try to take the high road every time. Of course, we've made mistakes and have regrets, but it's so important to focus on the positivity we can bring even when we disagree with people. When you're responding to a post, ask yourself if this will hurt someone else. Maybe someone posted a negative comment or link about someone. Will you adding fuel to the fire really change anyone's mind or will it just increase negative thoughts? Sometimes people stop commenting on the original post and just start name-calling or being mean to another commenter. Be sure you're staying focused on the initial comment or post and not getting caught up in a thread of crazy replies that just spin people into a spiral of ugly. We like to say, "Pretty is as pretty does." People can hate us for what we believe, and they are free to, but we will never give them ammunition by spewing the same hate.

Check the Facts

We hate that we even have to bring this up, but how often have you read a post and thought, "Is that true?" And you do a little checking to find out the story is false, but clearly the person who originally posted it didn't bother to check. It's like fake social media news—and it's not hard to do a little research. Also, there are a few satirical websites that post items that are supposed to be funny, but people post them without even realizing the source is *The Onion* or *The Babylon Bee*. Take a moment, catch your breath, and check the facts. By the way, it is okay to clarify that a post is satire or not true because it may save others from getting unnecessarily bent out of shape.

BiG StEpS

While the baby steps were mostly about you reacting and responding to others on social media, this is more about what you post. It may be your own posts or some replies to other people, but your words have power and we want them to build you up and not tear you down. Be proud of who you are and don't be afraid to state it, but be respectful of others as you do that.

Pass Through the Gates

Have you ever heard about the gates a thought or comment should pass through before you say it? The questions are: Is it true? Is it Necessary? Is it kind? If what you want to say can pass through each gate, you can say it without worry. That goes for posting on social media as well. We want to clarify that this does not mean you should only post things that everyone will agree with—not at all. However, make sure you are speaking truth and fact, that there is a need to share it and that it is not putting anyone else down. As an example, sharing the great things our president has accomplished while in office hits all of those buttons: 1. You only share the truth, and you can check your facts on www.whitehouse.gov; they list a lot of his accomplishments. 2. It is necessary because mainstream media purposely doesn't share any positive news about President Trump, so many people don't even realize all that he has done for us. We view it as our *duty* to let others know. 3. It's kind because you're sharing good news about the president, not putting anyone down. It's like a little gift to the uninformed. They can thank you later.

Share Things That Make You Proud

Focus on all of the good things you and your family are doing. If you and your kids took cookies to the police station, post a photo. If you visit a cool historical location, share the experience. If you voted, shout it from the rooftops. Sharing on social media about all the awesome patriotic things you and your family are doing puts out a very positive message. You will inspire other MAGA moms and share your caring heart for others in a very positive way. There's no need to start complaining if you're taking positive action!

Be Prepared and Move On

We covered this but cannot emphasize it enough. No matter how kind you are in posting, when it comes to sharing some traditional, patriotic, or Christian values, there WILL be people who are not receptive. There are people, like we said, trolls, who do nothing but look for the opportunity to spew negative thoughts and start arguments. Remember what we talked about in our chapter "Finding Your Voice"? Ask a lot of questions and listen. So, when you get that snarky comment and you feel like responding, ask them why they feel that way. You don't have to make a big deal about disagreeing with them; you can just state why you feel the way you do. The great thing is, because its online, you can prepare your response and don't have to react immediately. Also, and this may be the most important thing to remember when it comes to social media, know when it's time to move on to something else. You do *not* have to engage with angry people, and you do not have to argue your point. So, when you can tell there's no winning nor even a truce, just agree to disagree or ignore them and go bake some cookies with your kids!

Comments from the Choir

This is from Val. I definitely feel the least confrontational out of every-one in the group. Cjaye and Lyndsey, being sisters, are loud and proud and don't care what anyone thinks of them. I typically don't want to post anything that will maybe get negative reactions. People's opinions of me really get me down, and I tend to retreat and sometimes want to quit. This is an area I struggle in and I totally get why people would be reluctant to share their political views on Facebook or Instagram. However, Cjaye and Lyndsey remind me to focus on the positive and look at all the joy we bring to people by being bold and brave. It is an empowering feeling to be able to share your beliefs once you can tune out the negativity!

Notes

Notes

Notes

CHAPTER EIGHT

BEING PROUD AND BEING PRESENT

"When you open your heart to patriotism, there is no room for prejudice.
The Bible tells us, 'How good and pleasant it is
when God's people live together in unity.'"

—DONALD TRUMP

Someone recently said, "I miss September 12th." What they meant was, as horrific as the attacks on 9/11 were, and through all the losses, there was a time when every American came together as one. Members of the Senate and Congress, Republican and Democrat, stood on the steps and sang "God Bless America." Across the country, people reached out to their neighbors with a sense of true community. Citizens from around the world spoke kindly about America and remembered the many times we had aided their own country. For that moment in time, we were united. Yes, united in sorrow, but also stronger and kinder. When they said they missed September 12th, it wasn't the date on the calendar or the horrendous acts that came before. They missed the connection, the kindness, and the pride of the American spirit. It lasted for a while, but as always happens, people moved on with their lives. Sadly, there were other crises and acts of terrorism. Perhaps people were worn down with the day-to-day struggle of living. Whatever happened over the years, that feeling seems long gone. Today, not only are we more divided than ever, there is anger and outrage toward those who dare think differently. And, those who still love our country, support our president, and carry that American pride in their hearts are made out to be villains. The message we're told to uphold is no longer *Proud to be American* but rather *Guilty of Being American.*

Things seem a bit crazy, don't they? Forget about standing for the national anthem; the country is applauding those who kneel. Forget about wanting immigrants to come into our country legally and become citizens; we should open our borders and let anyone come in and take what they need. Freedom of speech and the right to bear arms are under attack. No wonder MAGA moms and families might choose to stay quiet and under the radar. You know the truth of who you are but might wonder if it's worth the backlash to stand up for yourself. Well, can we just say *yes*—it is worth it! Not only is it worth it; we need to do our part to be sure those great American values and freedoms are protected and embraced. We believe in everyone's right to voice their opinion—even if we don't agree with it. There has always been room for every side of an issue, so stand proud and speak out loud.

You can stand up for your faith and feelings, but you'll be more powerful if you do so in a kind and compassionate way. We believe when our words are wrapped in kindness, more people will hear our truth. It's like that adage, "You'll get more flies with honey than with vinegar." Haters out there will always think conservatives, Christians, Republicans, and all other patriots are horrible people. Yet, there are some great examples out there that show otherwise. One of our favorite examples of how to stand your truth in grace is Chick-Fil-A. It happened more than a decade ago, but the action still speaks volumes. A group of conservatives decided to have a Chick-Fil-A appreciation day in support of the company's Christian stance on marriage. In order to combat that, some gay activists decided to have a counter-protest. No one tried to shut them down; in fact, one restaurant in Kansas gave the protesters free chicken sandwiches and water. It sent a strong message of love despite differing opinions. Acts of kindness from someone perceived as the enemy make the most difference. Remember that you can and should be proud, but you can do it without putting others down. Where can you make a difference?

Things to Do

Each person reading this is going to have different ideas on how to show patriotism and how to be proud of the country and community. We applaud that because if it's not authentic and true for you, it won't come across as genuine. This isn't about changing who you are, but about showing your true spirit. As you read through our ideas, keep that in mind and listen to your heart. You can move forward from there and be present in the lives of others—even in the smallest way—and you will have a positive impact in the world around you.

BaBy StEpS

There are many small ways you can show your pride in our country and stand firm in what you believe. Yes, you'll need to step out and be bold, but you don't have to shout anyone down or confront anyone in the process. Here are a few brave steps you can take.

Put Political Signs in Your Yard

Let people know who you stand with and how you plan to vote. The yard signs are easy to get at the local headquarters for the candidate of your choice. And, if you're so inclined, you can order them online. Depending on where you live, you may have them stolen, but have you seen the ones that send an electric shock through people who try to steal your sign? Maybe invest in those! Seriously though, high road—remember? Just know that is going on and be ready with back up signs. Initially, you may feel like the lone wolf out there, but we know from experience that others who feel the same way will be encouraged by your example. Heck, they may even get some signs for their own yard! We personally have Trump 2020 bumper stickers on our cars. The plus side of this is that haters see you coming and let you through like the queen you are.

Invite Someone to Church

So many times, people are hesitant to go to church because they think it's full of perfect people and they know they are far from it. Listen, we go to church because we are imperfect people! Just invite them in and let them know Jesus does the cleaning. We're all messed up in there; if we weren't, there would be no need for Jesus in the first place. This is a great gesture you can use to meet a new neighbor or reach out to someone who is having a hard time. Just call them up to see how they're doing and then invite them to the next event or service at your church. People have been made to feel that doing this is shoving your religion down their throat, but that's not what you're doing at all. For all you know, that person may really be searching for some spiritual fellowship and isn't sure where they'll be welcome. And if they decline, that's okay; you've planted a seed. You can always let them know they're always welcome if they change their mind and then ask them if you can pray for them. Asking someone for permission to pray opens up the dialogue so much more than just saying, "I'll pray for you."

Adopt a Solider

This is another activity that can be done on your own schedule but can make a real difference in a soldier's life. Reach out to your local base, the USO, or some other military support organization and find out the guidelines for how to best encourage your military. Maybe you and your kids can write letters to a soldier or send care packages. And, if there are any welcome home events for your local military, make a point of being there. Not only does this remind our military that we appreciate their service, but it provides a great reminder to your kids on sacrificing for others. And, yes, we love the idea of posting photos from any military appreciation events and efforts online.

BiG StEpS

Okay, so we said the baby steps didn't mean you needed to do anything too public to show your pride. But there are some things we think are important ways to shout your patriotism from the rooftops. Again, this isn't about angrily confronting others. These are just a few ways you can be bravely patriotic!

Sing Your Heart Out

If you want to follow in our footsteps and use music as your voice, we strongly encourage you to do so. But even if you don't feel musically inclined, you can still sing. Whenever the national anthem is played, stand up and sing along! When you're at the ball game, or watching a parade, or looking at fireworks, sing all those patriotic songs and sing loudly. Who cares if you can't carry a tune in a bucket? That didn't stop us! You'll be singing from your heart! Plus, if you've been singing some of these songs around your house and with your kids, that's even better. This is a great opportunity to show your kids that it's okay to be American and proud of that fact.

March for What Matters

Sometimes we need to take to the streets. If there is a march or walk for a cause important to you and your family, walk along with others. Yes, this is a *big step* because you're out there in public where you can be seen by others, standing up for something. But if it's something you are truly passionate about, then why wouldn't you? Maybe it's a march or walk that's pro-life, or for freedom of speech at your local college campus. If you don't speak up, who will? Put on your comfy shoes, grab the sign, and stand tall! We personally support Women for America First, headed by Amy Kremer. She puts on a lot of great marches in support of our president in D.C. Follow her and maybe you can join us at one of them.

Stand Up for Your Opposition

This is something that can and will speak volumes to others. It's one thing to stand up for what you believe in; many will do that. Matthew 5:46–47 says, "If you love those who love you, what reward will you get? Are not even the tax collectors doing that? And if you greet only your brothers, what are you doing more than others? Do not even Gentiles do the same?" The challenge in these verses is to go beyond what is expected. When you can stand with an enemy or someone who disagrees with you, that action is kindness and the message comes through loud and clear. There have been stories of Muslims standing outside a synagogue to keep Jews safe during Sabbath, and Christians who stood in solidarity outside a mosque. It may not be that big and bold, but when you can stand up for your opposition, not only do they have their freedom of speech projected, but so do you. This will take some bravery, but when you see injustice and stand firm, you will stand tall.

Comments from the Choir

We are 100 percent pro-border wall and anti-illegal immigration, but that doesn't mean we don't have compassion for the people that come here. There are women and children that have been kidnapped and trafficked and then they end up detained for various periods of time. They are scared and away from their families. We often say we are pro-legal immigration, yet we'd be the first in line helping these people at a church or detention center if they were near our town. Our local church gathered items to donate to these facilities this summer. There is nothing wrong with loving the person even if you don't agree with them or their choices.

Notes

Notes

Notes

Notes

CHAPTER NINE

PRAYING FOR THE NATION

*"If we ever forget that we are One Nation Under God,
then we will be a nation gone under."*

—RONALD REAGAN

If you're anything like us, you always try to take care of things yourself. You don't ask for help because you believe you should be able to just handle this, handle that, handle everything! Then, we wonder why we get overwhelmed and burned out. The good news is there is something we can do about that. Perhaps we just need a reminder that the last thing we often do, is the first the we should always do—pray! It may seem the simplest action to take, but for Christians, it certainly has the biggest impact. This is especially true when it comes to what we can do to support and uphold our country with the values we believe in most. We watch the nightly news and see story after story of crime and corruption—people hurting each other, lying about others, and covering up when all else fails. It seems that too many of our leaders are out for themselves rather than working with our president to do what's best for the country—for us. We are left feeling hopeless and at a loss for what we can do. It's time for us to claim the mighty power of prayer that can touch the hearts of everyone—even if they don't know we're praying for them.

There is a never-ending discussion (or argument) on whether America was founded as a Christian nation. It's true that not all of our founding fathers were Christians, but the first American citizens were largely Christian. We were indeed founded in part for the freedom of religion and Christianity has always been deeply rooted in our collective values. For that reason, patriotism and love of God often go hand-in-hand, and conservative and Christian values usually align easily. We want to take pause here to clarify something. We do not judge or discriminate against other religions, particularly when it comes to what it takes to be an American. We believe all faiths should be able to worship freely, but we can only speak on the experience of our own faith. As Christians whose faith is our foundation, we often turn to prayer for our families and ourselves. Doesn't it then make sense that we should also pray for our nation? Maybe you already do this, or maybe you've never thought about it. Regardless, we can pray now and pray often.

Alfred Lord Tennyson said, "More things are wrought by prayer that this world dreams of." Prayer makes a difference in both the person doing the praying and the subject of prayer. When you need to calm your anxiety of how crazy things are, nothing can bring you peace like prayer. And when you believe in prayer, it can bring about miraculous things. The challenge for us, and we hope you'll take it up as well, is to pray more specifically and with more intention. Every prayer is powerful, so we have not separated our ideas into baby steps and big steps. Here are some specific ideas for how you can pray for our nation.

Pray for the President (and His Family)

This one is pretty obvious, but we suggest you take it beyond a basic prayer and focus on the specific issues he is facing on any given day. Pray for his insight, for his protection, and that he would hear God's guidance. Include his entire family in your prayers as well. Everyone in the first family has been targeted with hateful comments and actions. Hold them up in your daily prayers.

Pray Before You Vote

This isn't a daily prayer, but it's mighty important when election time rolls around. Ask God for His input and wisdom as you decide how to vote. Be sure you don't get so caught up in politics that you lose focus on who is really in charge. Pray you will make the best decision every time you vote.

Pray for the Opposition

Some days this may feel harder than others, but as a caring, compassionate Christian, it is important to pray for those who do not see things the way we do. This can be family members, friends, neighbors, local political leaders and those in Washington, D.C. Before you head off to any of your meetings and events, if you think you're likely going to face opposition, pray for them. It will help you see them as another valuable human being and not just an idea or perspective.

Pray for Understanding

This prayer can take on many levels. You want to ask for wisdom to understand God's perspective in the world. You should also pray that you will understand where other people are coming from and that you would have compassion for them. You do not have to agree with someone to be compassionate and understand the experience that brought them to their current perspective. And, the better you understand where someone else is coming from, the more likely you can have an open, caring conversation. Who knows, you may even change their mind!

Pray for Safety

Everyone wants to be safe and feel safe as they make it through this world. You can pray for the safety of our military, our first responders, yourself, and your children. One active way we've done this is every time we hear a siren, we pause and pray for the medics, firefighters, or police officers that they arrive safely to wherever they're headed. We also pray for the people waiting for help. If you've ever been waiting for an ambulance to show up at your home, you know how helpless these people feel.

Pray for Your Neighbors

Here's what we love about this one: you can easily put feet to it. Why not take a walk with your kids around the block and pray for each household as you pass by? It doesn't have to be a detailed prayer, just pray for their day, for blessings on them, or that they would feel God's presence. If you do know something specific that they're dealing with, absolutely include that in your prayer. We earlier talked about being truly kind to your neighbors; praying for them is one of the kindest things you can do.

Comments from the Choir

Our prayers can be big or small and they've shaped so many different areas of our lives, even ones people would deem insignificant, like our interactions as moms with other moms or big things like our children! We realize how hard it can be to pray for the opposition. Our pastor likes to joke that sometimes he needs to spit after he prays for someone he doesn't like! We realize we are all God's children and he cares for each one of us, even our enemies, the same. We are actually told to ask God to *bless* our enemies; how hard is that? This is something we struggle with because even in our little community, there are a lot of other moms who have chosen to hate us because of what we stand for. As easy as it would be to hate them back, we pray for them. We smile at them; we wave at them. We truly feel that God has guarded our hearts from allowing that to eat away at us. We know God is using us and the intimidation that comes from opposition is really the devil just working through them. We hope one day they can see our hearts are genuine and can be friends with us.

Prayer has also shaped the most important moments in our lives, like when Joey Belle was only three weeks old and went into heart failure. She had to have immediate open-heart surgery and let me tell you, we wanted the whole world to pray for her. We made a post on Facebook asking for prayers and you won't believe the amount of support and love that came flying our way. Even people who were not our friends prayed for her. Our "enemies" prayed for Lyndsey and Joey. They showed up. Thankfully our prayers were answered, and Joey Belle has a near-perfect heart now. If these prayers had not been answered, we would not have our little force in the pro-life movement and a huge reason why we wrote our pro-life song. Lyndsey literally cannot sing that song without crying it is so personal to her—and us! We like to think God is using Joey Belle to help other women choose life.

We even love the stories of prayer that have nothing to do with us but how they have affected our nation. In the movie, *The Trump Prophecy*, they started a nationwide prayer chain weekly to pray for President Trump, and would you look who is in office now! It seemed impossible to everyone; even the pollsters thought he didn't have a chance. That is the power of prayer right there. God literally takes the impossible and makes it happen.

Our prayers are for all of us, no matter what our differences are, to come together in heart and prayer for the betterment of all our individual lives and the great nation we are so blessed to live in.

Notes

Notes

Notes

CONCLUSION

*"I alone cannot change the world,
but I can cast a stone across the waters
to create many ripples."*

—MOTHER TERESA

There are a few things we want you to remember as you read through this book and find ways to express your patriotic spirit and defend God, family and country.

First, we cannot stress enough to chuck perfection out the window and just do it. Wherever you are in your patriotic journey and whatever you decide to try or not try, you're doing fine. Remember, we aren't professional singers; we just wanted to share our voices, our love of country, and our support of the president of the United States. So, we just turned on the camera and went for it. Yes, we've made mistakes, but we get better every day and our voices and reach are growing. We went from one video online to an entire movement! Imagine what you can do—just one step at a time. Make it *your* journey.

Second, all of this is really about your children and the kind of world you want them to live in today and going forward. Putting your country first *is* putting your family first. We're securing little futures, mama! There's a lot of pressure for not only parents but children as well these days. Kids are exposed to so much information at younger and younger ages. Sometimes it feels like they aren't allowed to be kids long enough.

The culture our kids are growing up in can not only steer them away from the Christian and family values you have, it can make life downright confusing as well. Our culture and habits are the reasons depression, medication, addiction and teen suicide are on the rise. We hope that our efforts can not only help change the dynamic in your family but also, change the perception within our country and show that MAGA moms and MAGA families are good-hearted, full of love, kind, and caring people. If we can raise up our children with that knowledge and solid foundation, maybe they will spread the roots that we have planted, then go out there and continue to change the world!

Finally, we hope we've been able to encourage you to be proud to be an American and to raise your children and your voice to the betterment of our country. We're all in this together and we need to remember that. We would love to hear from some of you about the things you're doing to create and live in a home of the brave! You know these three girls will be beside you, cheering you on every step of the way. We're not just Trump's cheerleaders—we are *your* cheerleaders! We're in this together, mama. Now go get 'em!

ACKNOWLEDGMENTS

To every person who has encouraged us, laughed with us, loved us, and supported us: we love you more than you know and we're so happy you are on this Trump train with us...working to Keep America Great! Toot toot!

To all the trolls: thank you for spending countless hours knocking us down and working for free...thank you for all the free publicity. You guys are better than any publicist we could ever hire.

To our families: thank you for putting up with the red singing hats, awful voice scales around the house, and the late-night song idea calls... it's amazing you still love us.

To Trump: thank you for stepping up, for using the nonstop negative MSM onslaught as fuel, for fighting for America's families, our religious liberties, our unborn, and our freedom. You make proud, make us laugh, and inspire us every day. Please never stop tweeting.

To Hillary Clinton: thank you for the name.

To Jesus: thank you for leading us, for loving us although we are so unworthy and sometimes suck, and for forgiving us. You know us Texas messes over here need major grace.

ABOUT THE AUTHORS

Cjaye, Lyndsey, and Val are three Texas moms who are passionate about God, their country, and their president. Seeing the culture crisis that gripped their nation, they found the boldness to start an online platform that gave them a voice, got them involved in the political process, and helped inspire others to do so as well.

Cjaye is a mom of three children, a professional diaper changer, and an admitted failure at potty training. Along with loving her kids, she loves dogs and with all of the crazy activity that brings to her home, she has embraced the fact that her house will always be messy. She's an overly passionate go-getter who refuses to quit once she gets started. She finds herself the unexpected lead singer of the Trump-loving band, The Deplorable Choir.

Lyndsey is a mom of two "wild-child" kids and three angel babies. Inspired, blessed, and encouraged by her daughter who has Kabuki Syndrome, she is a pro-life warrior and Kabuki Syndrome advocate. When not loving on her kids, she is a lover of impromptu dance parties, wine, and comfy leggings. Cjaye's sister, she is a background singer for The Deplorable Choir and serves as the band's Instagram story director.

Val is a mom of two children. And she is the life of every party. At most events, you can usually find her at the bar with a beer in hand wondering how, as someone who never sang before, she is a background singer and rock star with The Deplorable Choir. While perhaps the quietest of the trio, she is the loyal member who is always there when called to step up and stand tall.

Notes

Notes

Notes

Notes

Notes

Notes